BIG GOVERNMENT LOVE and YOUR MONEY

Exploring the Role of Government in the Economy

DAVID WESTROM

ISBN: 1477477454

ISBN-13: 9781477477458

Library of Congress Control Number: 2012909106

CreateSpace, North Charleston, SC

Table of Contents

Preface

The discussion and debate around the proper role and impact of government with respect to the economy is often positioned as complicated and confusing. We live in an age of sound bites, where people demand quick, concise answers to questions, regardless of whether the questions are simple or complex. Most people simply don't have the time for a history lesson, an extensive review of the Constitution, a long examination and debate on the intent of the founding fathers, or a deep dive into the underlying causes of the Great Depression. The many variables that are often introduced around government's role in the economy drive the perception that the issue is complex. Listening to debates, newscasts, or reading news articles that cover the issue can be a frustrating experience. I believe that, when properly framed, the issue is fairly simple. The purpose of this book is to provide that framing. While the roots of rapid government growth and staggering debt may date back to the Great Depression, the focus of this book is on the last forty years and the current generation, the decisions, the events, the overall thought process, and the facilitators that have led us to the edge of the financial abyss, where we stand today. This book explores and challenges an underlying philosophy, multiple assumptions, and a thought process, setting the stage for a debate that will hopefully catalyze positive change. The book will also offer ideas on how to reverse the course that we are presently charting, in a direction that takes us away from the approaching cliff of insolvency. The solutions I suggest are simple, and certainly not original. To understand this book, one only needs an open mind, common sense, and the ability to perform some basic arithmetic.

This book is dedicated to my mother, my late father, who always told me to use my head for something other than a hat rack, my son, and all of the other young adults and children in the United States who will ultimately be forced to foot the bill for, and deal with all of the extenuating consequences of, big government love.

CHAPTER 1

Introducing Big Government Love

'Tis not without reason that (Man) seeks out and is willing to join in Society with others who are already united or have a mind to unite for the mutual Preservation of their Lives, Liberties and Estates, which I call by the general Name, Property. The great and chief end, therefore, of Men's uniting into Commonwealths, and putting themselves under Government, is the Preservation of their Property. —*John Locke*

Many people believe that a major threat to our economic well-being and our prosperity as a nation is the unchecked growth of big government and the expanding role that it continues to play in our economy. The United States is presently experiencing stagnant economic growth, fewer jobs, lower wages, and an unsustainable, crushing debt burden that is leading us down a path to insolvency.

What is it?

What is big government love? It is the belief that big government is an all-knowing, all-caring, and loving provider that is duty bound to meet the perceived needs of the citizenry. Big government love is also a process of confiscating the working wage and accumulated wealth of private individuals, businesses, and future generations to spend on programs, goods, services, and entitlements that the government deems appropriate. The government's view of what is appropriate is based on the government's subjective view of what is "fair" and on what the government believes meets the needs of, and is in the best interest of its citizens and the country in general. This belief system and process is driven by a series of questionable assumptions that lead to a number of questionable conclusions. Americans are deeply patriotic and, with a very few exceptions, I believe that we all love this great country. But do we love the fundamental direction that this country has taken in the last forty years, a direction that consists of accelerated growth in the size, reach, and influence of government in the economic lives of all Americans? We love our country but do we love "big government love"?

Where do you stand?

What is your position on the role of government in the economy? A simple test along with the answers to a few basic questions will assist in discovering your position and personal views. Please take a dollar bill and take a long, hard look at it. How did you obtain that dollar bill? The answer for a great majority of Americans is that you worked for it. Now ask yourself this question: Who is more capable of making the decision on what should be done with the dollar bill that you are holding in your hand, you or your loving big government? You may be planning to save that dollar, invest it, give it to charity, or spend it. Whatever your intent, you choose how that dollar bill will be allocated or dispensed. Or, you may believe that the government is more capable of effectively determining what should be done with that dollar and that the government should be able to confiscate that dollar from you and determine how it should be *spent*. I emphasize the word *spent* because, as history has shown, the government intends on spending every dollar that it comes in contact with. The government doesn't like the term spend, they would prefer the term *invest*. In this book, we will investigate the government's track record when it comes to investments.

Next question: Who is more capable of making the decision on what should be done with a dollar bill that your neighbor or fellow citizen is holding in his, or her, hand? Do you believe it is your neighbor or big government? One would assume that the answer would be consistent with your previous answer unless you feel that you have some unique knowledge or a particular set of skills that perhaps your neighbor does not. Now ask yourself the following question: Who is more capable of making the decision on what should be done with a dollar bill that your child, grandchild, or the child or grandchild of someone you know will obtain sometime in the future—your child or big government? That question has already been answered for you because the government is spending the money today that your children and grandchildren will earn in the future.

Present Status

Today, the government borrows approximately forty cents on every dollar spent. The total accumulated debt of the United States is approaching $16 trillion and is forecasted to hit $20 trillion in the next few years (1). Assuming a population of 300 million, this equates to approximately $50 thousand in debt for every man, woman, and child in the United States. In 1992, United States debt stood at $4.2 trillion (2). The debt has increased by roughly four times in the last twenty years. In 2011, the United States took in $2.3 trillion in what government likes to refer to as revenue and spent $3.6 trillion (3). Our country had to borrow the $1.3 trillion difference or deficit from countries such as China, which will ultimately have to be paid back by future generations. This amount was added to the overall debt figure. The annual interest on the accumulated debt has also become a major budget item that steadily increases every year as we continue to spend additional money that we don't have. Annual interest presently absorbs approximately 6 percent of the overall federal budget (4). The $16 trillion total accumulated debt figure does not include government obligations for Social Security, Medicare, and Medicaid. The estimates for these additional obligations range from $40 trillion to $65 trillion.

Let's put this in perspective. If you had a job today that paid you $60,000 annually and you were in the financial state that the United States government is in, your annual expenditures would be roughly $100,000 and you would owe approximately $600,000. The annual interest payment that you would be making on your debt would absorb a major portion of your annual income. The bank would effectively cut you off from borrowing any more money, you would have to immediately cut your spending drastically, and you would probably have to sell any assets that you owned to pay your debt and sustain a minimal standard of living. You would effectively be insolvent and would probably declare bankruptcy. That is the real world. The difference between you and the government is that you don't have the ability to print an endless supply of money in your basement, and you don't have an endless credit limit. The truth of the matter is, neither does the government. At some point, the debt must be paid in one form or another. The strategy, at this point, is to keep spending ever-increasing amounts of money and kick the can down the road for future generations to absorb and deal with. Future generations would be your children and grandchildren. The theory is that all of this government spending will somehow accelerate the growth of the economy and generate more revenue for the government, allowing the debt to be repaid at some point down the road. The problem with this strategy is that you can only kick the can so far before people stop lending you money. There is also a built-in assumption that any additional government revenue would be used to pay down debt versus being spent. History shows this assumption to be false. History, along with present-day examples such as the financial crisis in Europe, provides a clear view of the financial implosion that is our ultimate destiny if we don't change course.

Back to the Question

The question regarding who is more capable of making the decision on what should be done with your dollar may appear to be subjective on the surface. But, in fact, it is not. With regards to the decision that is best for the individual, the small business, the big business, future generations, the economy overall, and even the government, there is only one logically correct answer regarding who is most qualified to dispense your money. The following chapters will examine the underlying beliefs, assumptions and logic used to answer this question from varying perspectives. The book will also explore the systemic drivers of big government love and the impact that it is having on our great country.

CHAPTER 2

What a Drag- Big Government and the Economy

I contend that for a nation to try to tax itself into prosperity is like a man standing in a bucket and trying to lift himself up by the handle. — Winston Churchill

-

The economy is the engine that produces wealth, which determines the collective standard of living of our society. The economy is made up of a number of components. This book will focus primarily on two principal components: the public sector and the private sector. The public sector is the government. It is funded from taxes collected from individuals and businesses. The private sector consists of individual consumers and privately and publicly held companies or businesses.

The Economy and Capitalism 101

The value of the goods and services produced in the economy, referred to as gross domestic product (GDP), is a direct measure of the health of the economy. If overall economic activity grows and overall revenue and profit increases, the government will collect more tax revenue. In a growing, vibrant economy, jobs are created, consumers spend, people invest in new businesses, and the overall standard of living of the country improves. If the economy slumps, the government will collect the same or less tax revenue than what was collected the previous year. What truly drives economic growth and a healthy economy? Some people believe it is the government, or the public sector. Some people believe the government creates jobs, wealth, and prosperity. Others believe it is the private sector. Still others believe it is a combination of both. An examination of what drives the private and public sector and how they function provides a better understanding along with an answer to this question.

Businesses in the private sector are owned by private individuals or groups of shareholders. These individuals or groups invest their money, time, and energy to create and grow a business. The business generates products or services and employs people in the process. The primary objective of the business is to return a profit to the investors who risked their time and money. Profit is the amount of money that remains after costs are deducted. In order for profit to occur, the company must develop and bring to market, in an efficient manner, a product or service for which the market has a need. The market is comprised of consumers, businesses, government, non-profit organizations, and so forth. If the market, for whatever reason, rejects the product or service, then the company providing that product or service does not generate sufficient revenue to cover its costs and make a profit. If a company in the private sector does not return a profit to its investors, it eventually goes out of business. If a successful, profitable company is unable to continuously innovate and bring value to its customers, another company may fill the void, creating a circumstance in which the previously successful company could be acquired or go out of business. This process is known as creative destruction (1). It is fundamentally how capitalism works, and it is the system on which our economy, which has been the envy of the world, was built.

Innovation is critical in a capitalist system as well-executed new ideas and business models create enormous amounts of wealth, jobs, and profits for investors. And once again, companies that fail to innovate fall by the wayside. The evolution of smartphone technology is a great example of this.

Companies that were once titans of industry are shrinking, reducing their workforce and, in some cases, going out of business, while other, more innovative companies are growing rapidly and producing wealth, not only for their shareholders, but for the government as well. On close examination, the capitalist system in the United States is a highly efficient and productive system. *Efficiency* is defined as an effective operation as measured by comparison of production with cost (2). *Productive* is defined as yielding results, benefits, or profits (3). Companies that do not produce the products and services that customers demand, in an efficient and productive manner, go out of business. Employees that aren't competitive and productive within those companies are often forced to find a new occupation, either within or outside of the company. This, more than anything, acts as a driver to align your talents to the needs within the economy. We are all created equal, but we all have different God-given talents. In most cases, people enjoy the things at which they excel and vice versa. One of the biggest challenges in life is discovering where one's true talents lie. On the surface, the capitalist system often appears harsh, and certainly things are not always fair. History is filled with examples of companies and individuals who cheat and take advantage of the system. There are also countless examples of people who are and were treated unjustly. As an overall system, however, there has never been a greater success story in the history of the world. No system has ever created a higher living standard for its people and lifted more people out of poverty, both within and outside of the country. And no system has ever driven a higher degree of wealth creation and rapid rate of economic growth.

The public sector consists of government and government employees. There is no free market. There is no market mechanism to determine the effectiveness and efficiency of the goods and services produced by government. Budgets are created annually for government departments with the primary goal of spending all of the money in the budget so that the budget will be maintained or increased the following year. The underlying driver in public sector budgeting is spending. How could you ask for a larger budget if you did not spend all of the money in the previous year? What are the incentives to be innovative, productive, or efficient? There are no investors, only politicians, lawyers, and taxpayers. This is not to say that government employees are not hard working and, in many cases, extremely effective and efficient. It is simply an examination of the system and its drivers. From that examination, the results logically follow. We will explore the federal government budgeting process in the next chapter.

Because of the very nature of the system, the private sector is inherently more productive and efficient than the public sector. It is also a much more effective and efficient allocator of cash or assets available for investment, also known as capital. For these reasons, if the goal is to optimize the overall rate of economic growth and new job creation, stimulating the private sector is the way you achieve that goal. Ultimately, the private sector produces the wealth that generates the tax revenue that funds the government that pays for the salaries and benefits of government workers in addition to presently defined entitlements for the entire citizenry.

What happens when additional capital is confiscated from private individuals, private businesses, and future generations in the form of debt, and moved into the public sector? Because capital is allocated less efficiently due to the inherent drivers of the public and private sectors, the result is distortions in the market and suboptimal performance and economic growth. The drag created on the economy through this confiscation and shifting of capital prevents the economy from generating the revenue and profit required to pay for increased government programs, services, and entitlements, let alone pay down the debt. When the overall economy does not grow at a minimal rate, new jobs are not created at a rate to support a growing population and new entrants into the marketplace. When capital is confiscated and moved from the private sector domain into the public sector domain, the overall economy and the standard of living of the country as a whole are negatively impacted.

Government Growth and Its Impact

The belief that big government is an efficient and productive allocator and consumer of capital is one of the foundational pillars supporting big government love. It is a faulty assumption, and a close examination of the explosive growth of government over the last ten years and its negligible impact on the economy serves to prove the point. The size of the federal government has almost doubled over the last ten years. The following chart illustrates the growth in annual federal government spending from fiscal year 2001 to fiscal year 2010 (4).

Figure 1- US Federal Government Spending from FY 2001 to FY 2010

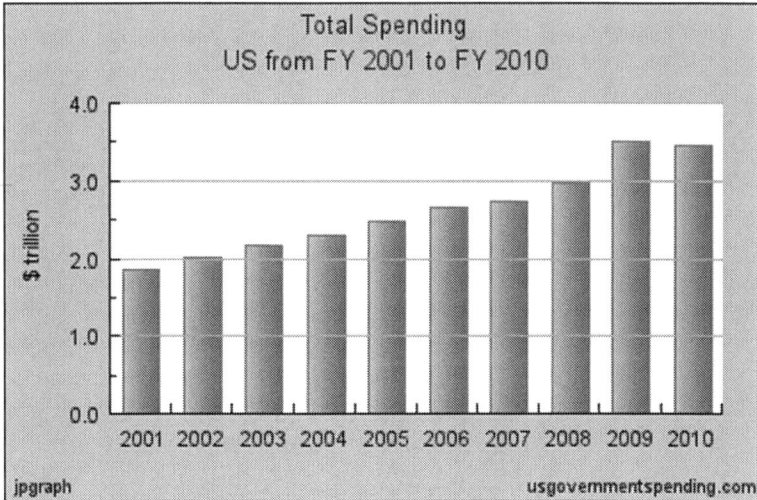

What is the result of that massive "investment" in big government love? Has that dramatic increase in government spending, which requires confiscation of wealth from private businesses, individuals, or future generations in the form of debt, resulted in rapid economic growth and a new age of prosperity? Not quite. Economic growth over the same period, as exhibited in Figure 2, has been anemic at best (5). As stated earlier, GDP represents the total market value of all of the goods and services produced by the economy of a particular country over a given period of time, usually a year.

Figure 2- US Real GDP 2001 to 2010

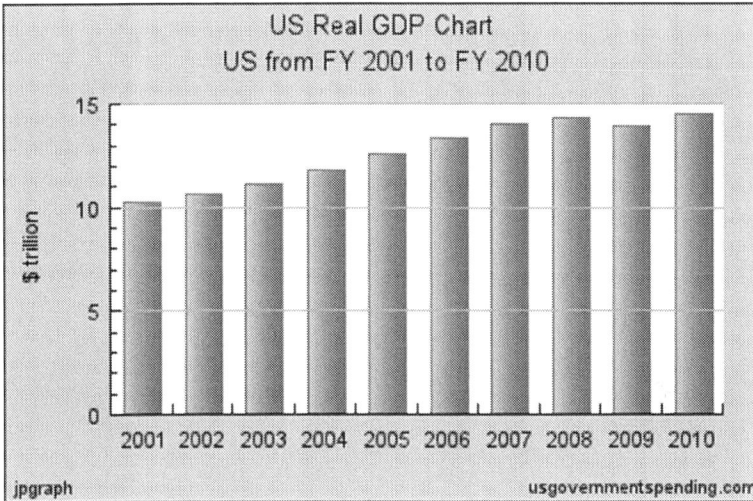

Since 2006, the United States has shown a rate of economic growth exceeding 4 percent in only one quarter (6). One could make a strong case that massive growth in government spending and the associated increase in debt, much of it occurring during this period, has, if anything, only served to retard economic growth and reduce the wealth and prosperity of the nation as a whole.

How do you simultaneously drive economic growth and reduce debt? You cut government spending and shift capital from government into the hands of private individuals and businesses. This shift of capital is accomplished through tax reform, tax cuts, and elimination of unnecessary regulations (and regulators) that place additional costs on the private sector and the overall economy. What about jobs that have been saved from all of the growth in government and government spending? The only jobs saved are government jobs and jobs that rely on the government for their existence. These are jobs that are deemed to be important by politicians, not the market. The question once again becomes, who is more capable of deciding how capital should be allocated, the politicians or the market (which is made up of you and me). What is clear is that many jobs have been lost over the last several years and the rate of new job creation has not kept up. Additionally, we have been left with a staggering debt burden that will be passed on to our children and grandchildren.

Big Gov Love: Department of Energy

Let's examine some specific examples of big government love. We'll start with the Department of Energy. This department was created during President Jimmy Carter's term with the goal of weaning the United States from its dependency on foreign oil. How do you think we are doing with respect to that goal thirty years later? Clearly, we are more dependent on foreign oil than ever. Any business in the private sector that proved to be such an abject failure with respect to its primary goal and objective would be disbanded and shut down. But let's look at what has happened with the Department of Energy. Today, it has approximately sixteen thousand employees, not including outside contractors, and has an annual budget of $29 billion (7). The department's budget has increased by approximately 40 percent over the last ten years (8). Can you tell me what they actually produce or what they are responsible for? How are they measured? I think most people are aware of their track record as an investor, or a venture capitalist, after the Solyndra debacle and their other green energy investments. The department does have responsibilities that are critical such as keeping track of the nuclear stockpile. The question is: how many people are required for that and at what cost? Also, does this functional responsibility of tracking the nuclear stockpile align with the charter of the department or should it reside in another department? The point here is not to pick on the Energy Department or its employees, who, I am sure, are wonderful, hardworking people. It is simply to illustrate, as an example, the suboptimal model and process that serves as the basis for how the public sector conducts business. The objective, and supporting business processes, are focused on fully exhausting a budget and incrementally growing that budget on an annual basis, regardless of the impact, efficiency, or productivity of the organization. It is all about politics and has nothing to do with anything of value as determined by the needs and demands of a free market. The winners in government are the ones who are able to maximize the increase in their budgets on a year-over-year basis. The foundation of this system is rooted in the Congressional Budget and Impoundment Control Act of 1974, which we will investigate in the next chapter.

Big Gov Love: Europe

Another example of the consequence of big government can be found in many of the countries in Europe. The European model is one that many in the United States aspire to and attempt to emulate. It should serve, however, as a warning of the potential damage caused by big government love. Over the last thirty years, many countries in Europe have shown dramatic increases in government spending, government entitlement programs, government debt, and the size of their public sector in relation to the private sector. This has taken place recently against a backdrop of economies that have experienced sluggish growth at best. In Greece, 14 percent of the working population has a job in government compared to roughly 8 percent in the United States. The unemployment rate in Greece exceeds 20 percent (9). The unemployment rate for the youth of Greece (age twenty-five and younger) hovers around 50 percent (10). Greek government debt is over 150 percent of GDP (11). You can find similar stories in countries such as Portugal, Italy, Spain, and Iceland. Not only are the huge entitlements, programs, and government services no longer sustainable by the private economy, the resulting accumulated debt acts as a crushing burden and restraint on the very growth that is required to cure the ailing patient. Many of these countries, after years of putting off the difficult decisions, have reached the point where they must cut government and the associated government benefits. But cutting the size and cost of government is extremely difficult for politicians because they believe that big government love is a good thing. So the debate now revolves around balancing government cuts with tax increases, which politicians love to refer to as "revenue" generation. Call it what you want but the simple truth of the matter is that it is additional confiscation of wealth from the productive component of the economy, the private sector. Tax increases on the rich, businesses, consumers, goods and services, and on property—anything to minimize the impact on the budgets of big government. Again, there is a belief by many within these countries that confiscating wealth in any form from an individual or business in the private sector will somehow help the economy and the country overall. A logical prediction is that the struggling countries in Europe that maximize the cuts in government spending, while reducing wealth confiscation or, at least, minimizing any additional wealth confiscation from their citizenry, will be the countries that ultimately see their economies, along with their standard of living, recover.

In the ongoing debate over the financial crisis in Europe, a common argument from those who support big government is that reducing government spending, or imposing government "austerity," has the negative effect of accelerating the decline of an economy. Many of the same people argue, as they do in the United States, that the real way out of the fiscal malaise is for the government to actually spend more, or "stimulate the economy." They also like to make the case that government spending as a percentage of GDP has actually declined in many of these countries over the last few years. It seems that measuring spending as a percentage of GDP serves as a convenient diversion; it is difficult to find the raw data showing the actual government spending numbers for many European countries. By creating this context, the implication is that government spending must somehow be linked to GDP. The simple fact of the matter is that year-over-year government spending has steadily increased in almost every European country over the last ten years. When the size of government, along with the debt that government incurs, becomes burdensome to the economy to the point where it negatively impacts healthy growth, many in Europe seem to believe that government still needs to continue to increase spending, just not as much. Reducing the rate of increased spending or spending the same amount as in a previous year hardly qualifies as austerity. Spain, for example, increased government spending by over 60 percent between 2001 and 2007 (12). In Spain, the real estate market expanded and government consumption expanded right along with it. But when the real estate bubble burst and the economy slumped, the government's voracious spending appetite certainly didn't burst along with it. The European Union uses taxpayer money, in this case German taxpayer money, to make loans to the banks because they are "too big to fail." The banks in turn use the loaned money to buy the government debt, artificially keeping the interest rates low. This allows the government to keep borrowing and spending money. When the bank funds run low, the government then lends the banks more money, and the cycle repeats itself. This process of treading water occurs against a backdrop of supporting the dead weight of government spending, which acts as an anchor, slowly dragging the economy down into the abyss. When GDP slows, continued growth in government spending, along with burdensome rules and regulations, impedes healthy growth and the ability to compete in a global economy. The real austerity is imposed on private individuals and businesses in the private sector through higher confiscation of their money to support a failed system. The Keynesian theory that the way out of a recession is for an out of control government to confiscate and spend even more fails not only the test of common sense but of history as well.

World Gov Love

There is big government love and then there is world government love, and that would take the form of the United Nations. The United States spends over $7 billion per year on the United Nations and related activities. The United States accounts for over 22 percent of the $13 billion plus budget, which includes their standard budget and extra-budgetary items (13). Why? What benefit do the citizens of the United States receive from spending $7 billion dollars that we don't have on the United Nations? The budget and spending of the United Nations has more than doubled over the last ten years (14). The United Nations presently has over 10,000 full time employees (15). So how does the United Nations spend our money? According to their most recent budget, their spending priorities are based on the following (16):

- Promotion of sustained economic growth and sustainable development
- Maintenance of international peace and security
- Development of Africa
- Promotion of human rights
- Effective coordination of human assistance efforts
- Promotion of justice and international law
- Disarmament
- Drug control, crime prevention, and combating international terrorism

Extra-budgetary items include categories such as "Peaceful Uses of Outer Space." Wow! That is quite an agenda. What I can't find in any of their records or official documents are any metrics that they use to measure progress or value in any of these areas. Perhaps good intentions are the only thing that we should be focused on.

Exactly, what is the United Nations? Should it be viewed as a charitable organization, a global law enforcement organization, a promotional marketing organization, a global advocacy or lobbying group, or a consulting organization? The United Nations charter states the following as primary goals (17):

- To save succeeding generations from the scourge of war, which twice in our lifetime has brought untold sorrow to mankind, and
- To reaffirm faith in fundamental human rights, in the dignity and worth of the human person, in the equal rights of men and women and of nations large and small, and
- To establish conditions under which justice and respect for the obligations arising from treaties and other sources of international law can be maintained, and
- To promote social progress and better standards of life in larger freedom.

These are clearly, noble and broad intentions. They sound good but are hard to quantify from the standpoint of determining if measurable progress is being made. Does questioning the efficiency and effectiveness of a government entity like the United Nations make you a selfish, uncaring, unsympathetic person? Should we assume that if the intentions of an organization are noble, the ability to efficiently execute those intentions and deliver some sort of measurable value should never be challenged or questioned? The conclusion of many who love big government is that people who challenge government organizations in any form simply don't care as much as they do. Perhaps there is another reason that many people are concerned with the out-of-control spending of organizations such as the United Nations. Perhaps they do care just as much as others about the intentions, but they also care about ensuring that their hard-earned money is spent in an effective and efficient manner. Perhaps they may also believe that there are other, more effective, alternatives for their money that could provide even more value for the intended beneficiaries.

Some may view many of the causes of the United Nations as charitable. According to the American Institute of Philanthropy, a highly efficient charity will allocate 75 percent of the contributions they receive directly to the targeted recipient or cause (18). Many people base their charitable contributions on how efficient the charitable organization is with the dollars that are donated. This would seem like a common sense factor that would influence a decision on whether to donate to a charity. How efficient is the United Nations? What are their specific initiatives and what metrics are used to measure the effectiveness of those initiatives? The answers to these types of questions are difficult to find. The out-of-control growth of spending within the United Nations organization is not difficult to find or understand. Governments always seem to be able to find a worthy cause and intention that requires more of your money, someone else's money, or the money of future generations.

One of the more publicized initiatives driven by the United Nations is the campaign against supposed man-made or anthropogenic global warming. The science around man being the cause of increased global temperatures was settled a long time ago, according to the UN Intergovernmental Panel on Climate Change (IPCC). The problem, however, is that the actual data doesn't quite support the thesis. Additionally, there are now many questions with regards to how the actual data was gathered and analyzed based on the release of internal emails of many of the government sponsored scientists. The lack of warming over the last decade, along with the failure of the data to support previous computer models, suggest that additional CO_2 may not have the level of impact on the environment that was previously forecasted. There is also a basic question regarding the overall percentage of CO_2 that man can actually impact. Some experts have suggested that if every person, factory, and automobile on the planet ceased to exist, the impact on CO_2 production would be less than 1 percent. The assumed cause of global warming has also been subject to renewed debate. One theory, scoffed at by the government-funded scientific community, suggests that global temperature is directly related to cloud formation rates, which is determined by subatomic particles from outer space called cosmic rays (19). The theory, known as the Svensmark theory, states that the quantity of cosmic rays that enter our atmosphere is directly related to the level of solar activity, or the quantity of sunspots and flares emitted from the sun. The cosmic rays determine the extent of cloud formation, which is directly tied to the temperature of the planet. My goal here is not to debate the cause and nature of global climate change. I am more interested in the drivers and objectives of the United Nations, governments, and politicians that have funded this crusade. If one accepts the assumption that man is causing dramatic climate change that will result in global catastrophe, then it logically follows in the mind of a big government proponent that big government must do something to stop this. The underlying assumption, of course, is that big government is the most capable entity of dealing with such a problem. And what is the solution? The answer is always the same, regardless of the question. It is always a concoction of new regulation, greater government control, more government spending, and more confiscation of revenue from private individuals, private businesses, and future generations of citizens, all in the interest of doing what is best for us all. The bottom line is that big government benefits from the supposed crisis. The scientists that generate the data that supports the thesis that results in the growth of big government are funded by the very same government that has a vested interest in the outcome. Perhaps this is why these same scientists scoff at theories that challenge their assumptions and conclusions. At the same time, the politicians that promote the new orthodoxy are also the ones profiting by investing in the companies that are being subsidized and promoted by the government, all under the guise of what is best for the people and the environment.

If Ted Turner and other patriotic Americans believe that the United Nations is an effective vehicle that enables their philosophical and charitable goals, more power to them. However, many do not agree for a number of reasons, including a belief that there are other organizations more deserving of their charity. They should also be able to decide how and where their dollars are allocated without being judged and stigmatized.

Tolling for Dollars

A great example of the lack of government efficiency and productivity is road toll collections. The state of Pennsylvania, for example, taxes each driver in the form of a toll for the pleasure and convenience of using the Pennsylvania Turnpike, which runs from one end of the state to the other. The job of the Pennsylvania Turnpike Commission is simply to collect money, but the commission loses money. They are actually so heavily in debt that without major changes, they may have to declare bankruptcy. They have a license to confiscate money from every driver who uses the road yet they lose money! How can you lose money when all you do is collect money? Leave it to big government to find a way.

The commission's balance sheet shows a steady increase in operating revenue up to $759 million in 2011 as a result of a progression of toll rate increases (20). However, in order to prevent Pennsylvania's governor from turning the turnpike over to private operators, the commission agreed in 2007 to pay the Pennsylvania Department of Transportation roughly $500 million per year to fund road repairs (21). This is an interesting piece of news since I always thought the money from collecting tolls went to road repairs. Apparently, that was not the case. The money collected went to employee salaries, healthcare, pensions, paying bureaucrats and politicians, and operating all of the buildings that you see about every ten miles on the turnpike. In 2006, the commission collected $610 million and eked out a small gain (22). But now that they have to allocate some of that money to actually fix roads, they are losing money at an extraordinary rate, despite continuously raising the toll fees. If you can't make money collecting money, how can you be expected to effectively and efficiently manage anything? Wouldn't it make more sense just to eliminate the tolls and allow people to keep and spend their money? At least this way, the government of Pennsylvania might actually make some money from sales taxes.

Confiscation of capital from private citizens through unnecessary road tolls is bad enough. Needlessly confiscating the valuable time of the private citizens and businesses that foot the bill for big government is worse. A recent return trip home with my family from a day at the New Jersey shore provides an example. My family, along with thousands of other families, was forced to crawl down the Atlantic City Expressway toll road for over an hour just to pay a three dollar toll. There was no accident or other road emergency causing the delay that we experienced, just a bottleneck that happened to be the toll collection booth. In the case of this highway and other toll roads, "customers" in the form of taxpayers pay an additional tax for the convenience of having their trip expedited. There are other roads that can get you from point A to point B without requiring a toll payment. You choose the toll road and agree to the tax with an expectation that you are going to save time. Government has a monopoly on the highway system and is providing a service in the form of convenience and time savings. When the provider of the service generates the bottleneck that causes a loss of time, who pays for it? Who is responsible for the loss of time and associated loss of production for thousands of taxpayers due to this particular form of mismanagement? The South Jersey Transportation Authority is not only confiscating three dollars of my money, they are now confiscating an hour of my time as well. For many, time is a valuable, scarce commodity. If someone steals your money, they may go to jail. But needlessly confiscating time, under the guise of supporting big government, is simply an "inconvenience". That is clearly how the government sees it. If the government were to place any value on my time whatsoever, how could they not quickly and easily conclude that one hour of my family's time is worth more than their ability to generate an additional three dollars? The South Jersey Transportation Authority could have cleared the bottleneck by foregoing the tolls (the cause of the bottleneck) and allowing traffic to pass unabated until the backup was eliminated. Modern sensor and communication technology allows them to determine the extent of a backup in real time and it was clear that they were aware of the backup based on the digital signs on the highway that informed drivers of the wait time from a particular point to the toll booth. The bottom line is that, in government, time has little value, and confiscating the time of a private citizen is not a concern, as demonstrated in this example. In the private economy, the demands of the market continuously challenge companies to provide an improved product or service in an efficient manner. If they fail, as judged by the customer, someone else comes along and takes their place. As the operator of an express highway, the primary goal of the service provider, the government in this case, should be to provide as high a quality of service as possible. Doing everything possible to ensure the safety of the customer should always be priority number one. Following that, an expedited travel experience should clearly be the primary objective as it is the reason that the customer chooses to take the toll highway and pay the additional tax in the first place. Expediting the travel experience for the customer should be the basis for all decisions, operating procedures and processes pertaining to management of the highway. This includes not only toll collections, but road maintenance and procedures for dealing with highway accidents as well. Unfortunately, the primary objective of a government agency or department is to fully consume a budget, not to provide extraordinary products or services, or control costs, or to value the time of their customers.

Paying Your 'Fair Share'

Finally, what about those evil rich people, the "1 percent" who don't pay their "fair share" of taxes? Shouldn't the government confiscate their money so that they will pay their fair share and we can bring down the debt? Today, the top 1 percent pays close to 40 percent of the income taxes collected by the federal government (23). Is that fair? Maybe or maybe not. The question in my view is irrelevant and simply a diversion designed to distract one from the fact that the government has no intention of bringing down the debt. They will only spend any additional revenue that comes in. History shows that the only way to get big government to pay down debt is to force it to do so by law. This, however, misses an even bigger point: *Additional confiscation of wealth from anyone, whether it is the richest man in the country or the biggest business in the country, will only have a negative impact on the overall economy.* The only way you can argue against this point is if you believe that the government can more effectively allocate that revenue than the individual or organization from which the money is confiscated. So, once again, who do you believe is more capable of making the decision on what should be done with the dollar bill that you hopefully still have in your possession, you or your loving big government? Evidence suggests that big governments are the most inefficient and unproductive users of capital on the planet. That has been the case throughout history and it remains so today. Yet, despite this, countless people advocate big government love. They believe that big government is the way to solve problems and make people's lives better. How do they arrive at this position and conclusion? We will explore this in greater detail in the next few chapters.

CHAPTER 3

Planting the Seed
The Congressional Budget
Act of 1974

Everyone wants to live at the expense of the state. They forget that the state wants to live at the expense of everyone. — *Frederic Bastiat*

The roots of big government love and the debate on the proper role of government in the economy began many years ago. From the framers of the Constitution to the events of the Great Depression, there have been numerous individuals and events that have impacted not only history but the present day debate and condition of our country. The context of this book, however, is a focus on the last forty years and the role of the present generation in arriving at the crossroads where we find ourselves today.

Getting to the Root

The foundation of big government love, in the context of this generation, can be traced back to the passage of the Congressional Budget and Impoundment Control Act of 1974 (1). This law was designed with a number of objectives in mind. One was to prevent the president from being able to impound or prevent the spending of funds appropriated by Congress. The other was to create a more effective, efficient process for federal budgeting. Like many of the best laid big government plans, the result has been almost the opposite of the intent. The act created the Office of Management and Budget (OMB), which became responsible for preparing projections of federal spending for the following fiscal year. What a great idea, or a conflict of interest, depending on your vantage point, to make the scorekeeper part of the government bureaucracy. Is it a surprise that government spending projections that come out of OMB are hardly ever accurate and are almost always "adjusted" upward over time? The projection of federal spending, per the 1974 budget act, is to be based on *continuing existing levels of government services from the previous year, at a minimum.* This is now referred to as baseline budgeting, which requires that spending from the previous year be carried over and treated as the "floor" for spending in the ensuing year. The spending floor is then required to be adjusted upward by several factors that could be viewed as devaluing the worth of the government services. Those factors would include inflation, cost of living increases, and other "adjustments" in resources to maintain a similar level of services. To summarize, baseline budgeting is inherently designed so that the budget can never be decreased. When the various adjustments are factored in, subsequent-year budgets would start at a minimum of 6 percent above what was budgeted in the previous year. This means that any "cuts" in the budget would come off of the adjusted baseline increase for that particular year. This effectively makes it impossible to truly cut government spending. The statistics that illustrate the increase in government spending since the passage of this law support this conclusion. Since 1975, federal government spending has increased every single year with the exception of a slight decrease in 2010. The 2010 anomaly is simply an offset to the colossal 2009 spending increase driven by the government economic "stimulus" program. Government spending increased once again in 2011 and the year-over-year increases are projected to continue ad infinitum. The $800 billion stimulus, which was sold as a one-time increase in 2009, served to enable an unprecedented new baseline for government spending, driving our deficit, and debt, to new heights. The increase in government spending in 2009 alone is almost equal to the total amount that the federal government spent in 1980. The following chart illustrates the growth in federal government spending since 1980 (2).

Figure 3- Total Federal Government Spending from
FY 1980 to FY 2010

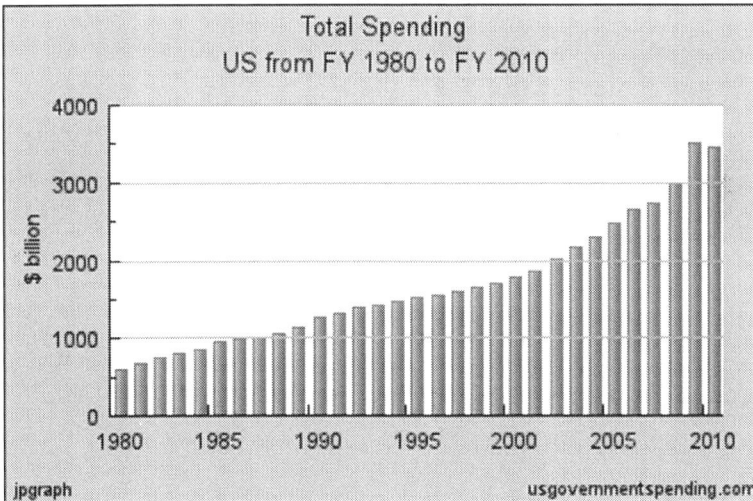

What makes the situation even worse is that when government politicians talk about cuts, they are talking about cuts that typically occur over a minimum ten-year period. As you can guess, none of the cuts will come until year nine or ten. And they are not really cuts. They are cuts off of the baseline annual increases built into the budget as a result of the 1974 law. So when a politician tells you that he is making $2 trillion of cuts, he is really saying that over the next ten years, but mostly in years nine and ten, we are going to spend $2 trillion less than we originally planned to spend, driven by a baseline budgeting process, which is almost double the amount that we spent in the previous ten years. Only in the whacky world of big government can this be said with a straight face. In the world most people live in, the definition of a spending cut is spending less money than the amount of money that was spent in a previous comparable time period which, in this case, would be the year before. In the world of big government, based on the budget act of 1974, a spending cut is spending less money than the automatic built in spending increase.

Baseline budgeting should also be viewed from the context of how it positions the process of budget negotiations and sets a distorted playing field for the debate on spending in Washington. The negotiation is always based on debating an appropriate and "fair" increase in spending *above* the built-in baseline increase. The baseline increase is viewed as no increase at all. If you are willing to enter into a debate on the amount of additional spending above the baseline, you are viewed as a moderate, reasonable, willing to compromise, or perhaps even a maverick. If you take a position that spending should be cut from the baseline increase, but still increased above what was spent the previous year, you are viewed as unreasonable and not willing to compromise for the good of the country. If you take a position that spending should be cut, as in cut from the amount that was spent the previous year, you are viewed as radical and draconian.

Shedding Some Light

The problem is that most Americans are unaware of the 1974 budget law and the underlying mechanisms that build in an increase in big government spending every year without referring to it as an increase. And the big government loving news media will never take the time to expose this convoluted process. Have you ever seen an investigative report on this law and its foundational role in the creation of the fiscal mess we find ourselves in today? Is it any wonder that the traditional news media in this country is viewed as the promotional marketing arm of big government?

A simple solution would be to abolish the 1974 law and institute zero-based budgeting, where the baseline for the following year is zero and the budget has to be built from the ground up based on a minimal set of requirements. That way, any cut will truly be a cut and not the manipulation of facts and figures by a smooth-talking politician. And one other suggestion: government spending should not be increased year-over-year by one penny until the debt is paid off.

CHAPTER 4

Love is Smart and Caring

I sit on a man's back, choking him and making him carry me, and yet assure myself and others that I am very sorry for him and wish to ease his lot by all possible means—except by getting off his back. — *Leo Tolstoy*

Why do people advocate an expanded role for government in the economy? What are the foundational beliefs behind the support for big government love? Let's go back to the basic question that we asked in Chapter 1: Who is more capable of making the decision on how a dollar that you earned should be allocated, you or your loving big government? How do you arrive at the conclusion that the answer is big government? Aren't you capable of making the decision with regards to your own money? You are the one responsible for your welfare and that of your family, aren't you? The answer lies in the core belief that the people in charge of government are smarter and that they care more. If you believe that government is smarter and cares more, then it makes logical sense that government should be able to confiscate people's money and spend it for them.

Smart

If you accept the notion that historically, the positive impact of big government on any economy has been minimal at best, why would anything be different now? Perhaps the people in charge in the past weren't the brightest. Perhaps they weren't the beneficiaries of hindsight and lessons learned over the past few hundred years. Or perhaps they didn't have the opportunity to attend universities like Yale or Harvard. Perhaps if the people in charge were just a little bit smarter, big government would work better after all.

Perhaps if (fill in the blank) were in charge, a new era of prosperity would dawn. So, who is the person or people that could make government effective and productive? In the era of television and the Internet, the media has promoted the perception that the smartest person in the room is the one who speaks well and does well in debates. Who are the best speakers and debaters? Why, it is the best lawyers, of course. Lawyers are trained not only in the law, but they are trained to be professional speakers and debaters as well. But does this make them the most qualified to run government and make decisions on how your money should be spent? Does it make them more qualified than you?

Why do so many people accept the assumption that a good debater is a smart person who is capable of taking a leadership role in managing the economic engine and the finances of this country? We have all seen convincing debaters who are factually incorrect on half of the content that comes out of their mouth. But they sound good saying it. Albert Einstein was smart. Was he a good debater or speaker? For all we know, he may have looked like a bumbling fool in a political debate. Does that mean his money should have been confiscated and spent by loving big government?

The fact is that everyone is different. We all have special talents and unique needs. What is best for you and your family may not be what is best for me and my family. The best school for your child may not be the best school for my child. The individual choices you make, the food you choose to eat, the people you associate with, the hobbies you enjoy, the charities to which you contribute, these are all decisions that are personal based on your own set of beliefs and requirements. Liberty and freedom allow us to make those decisions and be responsible for those decisions. An efficient, free market accounts for our unique requirements and choices, drives innovation, and optimizes the production and delivery of goods and services to meet the collective demand. The government distorts the proper functioning of a free market by imposing their own view of what people need and require. And when it comes to having a positive impact on the overall health of the economy, we are more effective and impactful in allocating our own money than the government. The idea that someone else is smarter and knows better is simply a false assumption.

Caring

Being smarter isn't the only requirement for confiscating other people's money and determining how it should be spent. Big government love is also based on "caring." People that love big government have the market cornered on caring. They simply believe that they care more than the rest of us and because they have the need to act on those caring feelings, big government becomes a means to an end. This deep caring is accentuated by a belief that people are fundamentally victims of circumstance and their environment, and that it is a basic obligation of society to take care of people that are perceived, by them of course, as victims. Being smarter clearly makes one more qualified to determine who is categorized as a victim. People who are victims really can't be held responsible for their actions or the situation in which they find themselves, so the government must chip in and help them in every way possible. If a person can be categorized as a victim, it then logically follows that they should be helped and supported by the government. This, of course, requires confiscation of more of your money. The problem with this logic, outside of the obvious arrogance, is the fundamental belief that government can effectively and efficiently help and care for people.

Noble Intentions

History is littered with thousands of examples of large, centrally managed government bodies extending their reach on their citizenry with the best of caring intentions and the same result: a lower standard of living and heavy damage inflicted on the people. The intentions always start out as noble. Let's look at the old Soviet Union for an example. In the Soviet Union, just like anywhere else, people needed to eat. Yes, we should all be able to agree that people need to eat. But would you pay twenty dollars for an apple? When loving big government decides they need to take over the food supply chain to ensure their caring objective, the result is disaster, as collectivization in the old Soviet Union so aptly proved. Many other countries today continue to follow their example despite the history of poor results. They are convinced that they can make it work because they, and their friends who help them run things, are smarter and they care more. People need to eat and people need healthcare. Starting to sound familiar? When the private sector is left to manage the supply chain, innovation, efficiency, and productivity are the drivers. The landscape is vibrant, dynamic, and ever-changing with new companies, products, services, and business models emerging every day. Pricing of products and services is optimized by the free market. Innovative private companies create new jobs. These companies also give back to their communities both directly and through their employees. Private individuals give back through charitable contributions to the organizations of their choice and through direct community service. Government plays an important role in enabling a healthy business environment by setting and enforcing some basic rules focused primarily on protecting property rights. But they play no further role in generating the growth and prosperity that arises from the market. When they decide that they, in their infinite wisdom and caring, need to participate in the market, control the market through over-regulation, or completely take over the market, they only impede its health and growth and negatively impact the benefit and wealth generated by the economy overall.

A Logical Conclusion

If I believe that I am smarter than you and care more than you, and I also believe that people are fundamentally a victim of circumstance, doesn't it logically follow that I would believe that it is my duty to confiscate your money and spend it for you. It is only logical that big government, in its wise, caring and loving nature, is much more qualified and capable of spending your money and taking care of you and others. In order to spend your money, they first need to confiscate it.

But what about the poor historical track record when it comes to the performance of big government involvement in the economy? In the view of many big government advocates, an example of a poor performing government was simply the result of the people running it being incompetent or corrupt. Perhaps they just didn't possess the knowledge and education that we have today. Could it possibly be that big government love represents a failed system? Perhaps the countries that are perceived as failures just didn't confiscate and spend enough. This is becoming a common refrain as the evidence of continued government lack of performance mounts. The only reason it didn't work or is not working is because the government didn't go far enough. They didn't confiscate enough and they didn't spend enough quickly enough. If only the stimulus would have been bigger, the economy would have recovered quicker. If we have another round of stimulus, the economy will surely recover and grow rapidly. If those rich people would pay their fair share, the economy will take off and loving big government can help more people. It is quite an interesting position to take since theoretically, you can never be proven wrong. The question is, how much money does loving big government want, or need, to confiscate and spend? How much money is enough? The size of government has roughly doubled in the past ten years, we borrow forty cents on every dollar we spend, and we are $16 trillion in debt and growing. But that is not enough. There is no amount that will ever be enough. Big government's appetite for your money is insatiable and big government will always need more so that it can continuously bestow more love on us.

CHAPTER 5

Laws and Lawyers
Big Government and Big Business

*Lawyers in making laws favor laws that make lawyers a
necessity.* — *Elbert Hubbard*

Who benefits the most from new laws and regulations? Why, lawyers of course. The result of every new law and regulation that is passed and implemented by the government is an additional compliance burden on individuals and businesses, which translates to greater expense. This has a direct relationship on the overall health of business activity and the economy, along with impacting the ability of a business and the economy to operate in an effective, efficient, productive, and competitive manner. The financial benefit associated with new laws and regulations flows directly to lawyers. New regulations drive new litigation, more compliance related consulting fees, and additional consulting advisory fees focused on adjusting practices and business processes. This is not to say that all laws and regulations are bad. Rules and regulations are needed to protect consumers and their property rights, and ensure healthy, fair competition in the market. There is a point, however, where the financial burden and negative impact on the overall economy outweighs any perceived good that may arise out of a newly enacted law or regulation. And oftentimes, the unintended consequences may also outweigh any benefit. The point is not to debate or judge whether specific laws are beneficial to society and the economy. The purpose of this book is to examine the role and impact of our government on the economy along with the underlying causes and drivers that have led to our deteriorating overall financial condition. The proliferation of rules, regulations, and litigation certainly contributes to the problem as it, more often than not, adds costs and impacts the ability of the economy to operate in an efficient and effective manner.

The United States of Litigation

It is no coincidence that the United States is the most litigious country on the planet as it has the most lawyers. Of the 535 members of Congress, almost half are lawyers compared to less than 1 percent of the population that are lawyers (1). We have already discussed how the news media have conditioned the populace to associate intelligence with the smooth-talking lawyer. What we haven't explored is the actual cost of all of this lawyering, the impact on the economy, and the negative impact of applying the thought process of a group of lawyers on the management of a budget, a balance sheet, or anything relating to business, finance, or economics for that matter.

Lawyers are trained to defend, to prosecute, to debate, to convince, to rationalize, and to argue. One could argue, however, about whether they are ever trained in mathematics or if they are taught basic budgeting, finance, and economics. I am going to assume that they are taught these skills, at some point, as they have families and budgets of their own that they have to manage. It is the other skills, however, that seemingly take over when it comes to governance and management of the people's money. What other conclusion can you draw when you have a senate that is unable to create a budget, when you spend over one trillion dollars more than you take in on an annual basis, and when you have racked up roughly 16 trillion dollars in debt, most of it in the last ten years? Only lawyers could turn the term *spending cut* into something abstract, subjective, and debatable through the Congressional Budget and Impoundment Control Act of 1974, making a spending increase really a spending cut if it falls below an artificial increase based on a number of factors that ensure fairness. In the wonderful world of politicians, anything can be rationalized, debated, twisted, repositioned, reconfigured, altered, modified, or simply changed in the name of fairness or some other abstract, subjective term that is also subject to the same rationalization, twisting, repositioning, modifying, altering, and so forth. In math, science, and engineering, there are numbers that are quantifiable and measured. In politics, there is no black and white, just multiple shades of gray.

It is difficult to determine the actual cost of government regulations. Some studies have shown that the cost of regulatory compliance imposed on Americans and American businesses exceeds $1 trillion per year (2). What is truly amazing is that a cost/benefit analysis is difficult to find as part of the normal course of business in developing new laws and regulations (3). When laws and regulations are passed that either don't work or are not enforced, why does the government pass additional laws and regulations on top of the ones that don't work or are not enforced? How many laws and regulations have actually been eliminated over the last thirty years? My guess is very few if any at all. New laws and regulations continue unabated, driven by the government's view of the issues and the need of the day, with seemingly no concern on the effect or impact on the economy and the people who pay the bills. The result of this abundance of government wisdom and love is an additional anchor tied to an already overburdened, sinking economic engine.

CHAPTER 6

Straw Men and Non Sequiturs and Red Herrings! Oh, My!

You can fool some of the people all the time, and all of the people some of the time, but you cannot fool all of the people all the time. — *Abraham Lincoln*

How does one make the case for a continued activist role for the government in the economy? How does one make the case for additional government spending? How does one make the case for continuing to spend money that we simply don't have? How does one make the case that we need to confiscate more money from private individuals and businesses? How does one make the case that we need to confiscate more money from our children and grandchildren? How does one make the case for big government love? In this chapter, we will examine the thought process, reasoning, and underlying strategies and tactics that support big government philosophy.

The Case Against

The argument against big government love is framed and presented in a concise manner in this book. It is based on statistics that are easily obtained and a few basic, fundamental principles:

- You shouldn't spend more than you can afford, and that also applies to big government. You certainly don't spend 40 percent more than you take in when you are $16 trillion in debt.
- The money that you make and the wealth that you accumulate as a private citizen, business, or investor is yours, and you are more capable than the

government of allocating it in a way that is more impactful to your family, your community, your business, the economy, and the government, than the government itself.

- You care enough and are smart enough to determine how your money should be allocated.
- The built-in drivers of big government make it inherently inefficient and unproductive when viewed in the context of the private economy.

The linkage of these points along with the statistics, examples, and recent historical evidence presented in this book support the position that confiscating revenue from private individuals, private businesses, and future generations and transferring it to big government results in a drag on economic growth and limits the ability of society to economically prosper.

A Fallacious Recipe

A position or argument is developed by presenting underlying principles, ideas, statistics, and examples, and showing a logical thought process and linkage of ideas to arrive at a conclusion. The validity of any position, however, is only as good as the foundation on which it was built. Challenging a position requires challenging the assumptions and the logic process that one uses to arrive at a conclusion. This focus attempts to minimize the emotional component embedded within a position and maximize the emphasis on the facts, statistics, and logic. Ideas, data, information, and analysis are exchanged with the goal of increasing one's knowledge and evolving a thought process. If the facts or underlying data changes, or the logical linkage of the facts and ideas can be successfully challenged, one should have no problem changing their position. Unfortunately, much of the discourse we see today is not driven by a logical process.

How do you support a position that big government is an effective and efficient allocator of confiscated capital when it is difficult to find any evidence in support of this position? The position is developed much like a recipe. The basic ingredient is the foundational principle that government is smarter and cares more, as presented in chapter 4. This is then supplemented with a concoction of illogical approaches and psychological tactics that have been around for a very long time. You might start with a false assumption or a statement that is built on an invalid inference. You could then choose to mix in an association of ideas that are not logically related, complimented by adding a generous dose of emotion that incorporates a strong "feeling" of what is "fair." The word *fair* is commonly used by those who support an activist, ever-expanding role for government in the economy. It is a word that evokes emotion and is totally subjective. What is fair to one person may not be fair to another. Who ultimately decides what is fair and what is not fair? We answered that question previously- it has to be the person that is the smartest and cares the most.

A Touch of Anomaly

Meeting our energy requirements and reducing our dependence on foreign sources of energy is crucial for driving sustainable economic growth. The extraction of natural gas in the United States through a drilling technique known as hydraulic fracturing or "fracking" provides a means for leveraging our own energy resources, creating jobs, and growing the economy. When standard safety and operating procedures are followed, fracking has proved to be an effective and environmentally sound method for developing our energy resources. A concern commonly expressed among opponents of fracking involves the potential tainting of the water supply. While this concern is certainly valid, the Environmental Protection Agency (EPA) has yet to document a case where fracking has tainted groundwater (1). Should we accept the argument that if there is even a remote possibility that something negative might occur in the future, we should not proceed with initiatives that positively impact our economy? Let's take this argument one step further and assume that there does exist, or sometime in the future, there will exist an example somewhere of fracking causing a tainting of the water supply. Then, a position could be established as follows: *Fracking may help the United States achieve energy independence but I am against fracking because in Blanktown, USA, fracking caused a tainting of the water supply.*

In this case, an anomaly provides the basis for the position. An anomaly is simply defined as a deviation from the norm. The use of an anomaly as the basis for a position or argument can be used as a foundation to support the idea that big government is the only one that can be trusted to address and solve problems. The strategy is often applied as follows: if a program, cause, or initiative can potentially yield any result that could be perceived as negative or abhorrent, even if that result occurs at a very small rate or percentage of time, leverage that anomaly to take a position where it would never happen at all, despite the fact that the contrary position results in an outcome that may be of great benefit to the economy and society in general. This leads to the ultimate conclusion that the government either needs to control the particular initiative, or perhaps even the market, in totality or impose a maximum amount of regulation to ensure that the anomaly will never occur. The anomaly strategy is often applied to support various environmental causes where, if any damage can be found to the environment or any type of animal or plant species, the resulting action has to be total cessation of the activity that is causing the perceived damage, regardless of the amount of the damage or the benefit of that activity to society. An example of this was cutting off water to Fresno, California, farmers to protect the delta smelt. The delta smelt is a tiny fish found in California that is on the endangered species list. Smelt were getting caught in water irrigation pumps and dying. The solution was to cut the water off to the farmers, protecting the smelt (2). The result for farmers, and the overall economy, is lost income, wages, and jobs. Could another solution have been found that may have helped the smelt without sacrificing the well-being of the farmers and damaging the economy?

The following provides another example of a similar nature: *Off-shore drilling, even though it contributes to our energy requirements, should be banned, because it can lead to oil leaks, like the BP disaster, polluting the ocean.*

Yes, off-shore drilling leads to oil leaks, and I think every-one would agree that polluting the ocean with oil is a bad thing. Do you adopt a position that if a BP disaster occurs, or if any oil leakage occurs, or a small percentage of oil leak-age occurs, off-shore drilling should be banned or enough regulation imposed so that drilling will either cease or move to another country? The better question may be, Why are companies drilling so far off-shore and in deep waters, which presents a much greater risk, when that risk, and any associ-ated damage, would be greatly reduced by drilling on land or moving closer to the coast in more shallow water? We don't drill in shallow water because it might impact the beaches and the fish. We don't drill on land because there is a chance it might impact people and the animals. Unless we can be 100 percent assured that an oil leak and any resulting damage will never occur, we should just never drill at all. This is where the line of logic always ends with big government as the defender and enforcer. Ensuring the total elimination of the anomaly, whether real or imagined, becomes the ultimate goal and ob-jective with economic well-being and overall standard of liv-ing being the sacrificial lamb.

A Cup of Non Sequitur

Leveraging a negative anomaly is one tactic. Leveraging a fallacy is another. A logical fallacy is known as a non se-quitur (3). A *non sequitur* (Latin for "it does not follow") is defined as an argument in which a conclusion does not follow from its premises (4). A position in which a premise is totally unrelated to the overall position is also considered a non sequitur along with a response to a statement that is totally unrelated or disconnected to the statement. An example of this is as follows:

Jane: Based on the amount of money our government has to borrow, I think government spends too much and needs to cut back.

John: Jane, you are wrong because government cares more and needs to take care of people.

When a conclusion is not a necessary consequence of a premise, or a series of premises, the position is a non sequitur. Even when the premises may be true, the conclusion may not be a necessary consequence of the premises. The logic is either faulty or deceptive. An example is as follows:

People need access to loans in order to be able to buy a house. Banks discriminate against potential home buyers for a number of reasons. Therefore, government must intervene to ensure that people who could be discriminated against have access to loans to buy a house.

This is an example of a series of premises that may be regarded as true being linked in such a way to form a deceptive conclusion that supports a greater role for big government. People do need access to loans in order to buy a house. Banks do discriminate against potential home buyers for a number of reasons including their income, job history, credit history, and so forth. Does it make sense to link these two statements together and conclude that the government needs to interject itself? This line of faulty logic, along with a perceived view of fairness, provided the basis for the housing collapse that we are still dealing with today.

Let's come back to the fundamental issues addressed in this book. The government spends more money than it takes in, is deeply in debt, and is inherently inefficient and unproductive. These statements are supported by logic and statistics that have been presented in this book. A common response proposed by proponents of big government who have no interest in cutting spending is the following:

> *The government needs to confiscate more money from rich people because they don't pay their fair share. They also would not be in the position that they are in if it wasn't for the fact that they are citizens of this country. They have leveraged the resources (roads, bridges, police, schools, etc.) of this country to make themselves rich. So they should pay their "fair share" (meaning more), and help bring down the debt.*

But this emotional diatribe is filled with non sequiturs, has no logical relationship or linkage to the overall position, and is not a viable solution to the problem. If you confiscated all of the income of the so-called rich, the country would still be grossly in debt. There is also no evidence to suggest that any confiscation of wealth would be used to pay down the debt. As a matter of fact, the evidence supports the opposing position. Additionally, there is no evidence that this confiscation would have a positive impact on the economy. Once again, the evidence suggests the opposite. The idea that success is somehow linked to the utilization of common assets, resources, and services that are funded by taxpayers is not only a false assumption but it is also a direct attack on liberty. It suggests that success and the accumulation of wealth is a direct result of the impact of big government and that big government ultimately has a claim on such success.

A Presidential Non Sequitur

President Barack Obama recently made a similar argument during his March 31, 2012, weekly address by posing the following questions: "We have to make choices. When it comes to paying down the deficit and investing in our future, should we ask middle-class Americans to pay even more at a time when their budgets are already stretched to the breaking point? Or should we ask some of the wealthiest Americans to pay their fair share?" (5) The president went on to say, "Either it's going to add to our deficit, or it's going to come out of your pocket. Families who are scraping by will have to do more because the richest Americans are doing less. That's not right. That's not who we are. In America, our story has never been about what we can do by ourselves—it's about what we can do together." (6) The president's underlying premise and goal, as shown in the second sentence of the quote, is that we need to reduce the deficit and invest in our future. I would agree and I assume that most Americans would agree with this assessment as well. The president goes on to present only two options for achieving that goal, confiscating more money from middle-class Americans or confiscating more from wealthy Americans. The assumption, based on the presentation of the argument, is that these are the only two options for achieving the stated goal. That assumption is false. If we want to reduce the deficit, could we not ask government to dramatically cut spending? And I mean really cut spending, not just spend a little less nine years from now than they had hoped to spend. How about asking rich people like Warren Buffett and Bill Gates' father, who apparently believe that the government is an efficient allocator of their capital, and other citizen's capital, to voluntarily write the government a big check? Also, why is "investing in our future" always equated to government spending an even greater amount of our money? Cleary, the government has not proven to be a very wise investor. The question and the argument are not framed in a manner in which multiple options are evaluated and considered with the intent of selecting what is most effective. The underlying assumption built into the president's position is that if we believe in investing in our country and reducing the deficit, we must allow the government to confiscate more of someone's money and the government must determine how to best allocate it. The underlying belief is the government is clearly most qualified to make the determination on how confiscated wealth is spent. The only open question is whose money do we take, and we are presented with two choices. Given the two options presented, confiscate from rich people or middle class people, of course you are going to select rich people. If you buy into the underlying assumptions and the options presented, then you are led to the conclusion that the president wants you to arrive at. And finally, he summarizes by stating that it is not about individualism, it is about collectivism, with government, of course, being in charge and calling all of the shots. The underlying argument is broken down as follows:

- The country needs to invest and reduce the deficit.
- The country needs to confiscate more money, or generate more "revenue," in order to accomplish this.
- It is better to take from the rich instead of the middle class or the poor.
- Therefore, we must confiscate more from the rich.

The problem with this argument is that, in addition to the underlying assumptions being false and the available options being incomplete, there is no logical linkage to the goal. This makes the argument a non sequitur. We can agree that if you are going to confiscate money from someone, it is better to confiscate it from a rich person over a middle class person. The problem is that confiscating additional money from a rich person, or any person or group of people for that matter, will not bring down the deficit or the debt and will not lead to "investment" in America. It will lead to less efficient allocation of capital in the economy and more government spending, which will simply result in less jobs, slower economic growth, and greater debt. There are other options for achieving the goal but they are purposely not presented.

A News Media Non Sequitur

A recent article from the editorial board of one of the nation's largest newspapers used a report giving states poor

marks for good governance as a vehicle to argue for continued big federal government spending and management of
"important" programs (7). This would also be categorized as
a non sequitur. The underlying assumption is that the largest
of all big governments is more efficient and effective than
smaller "corrupt" state governments. Of course they provide
no statistics or data to support their position. They simply use
a report that accuses state governments of being unethical
and poorly run to arrive at their conclusion. I must admit to
being surprised that this particular newspaper editorial board
would admit that any centrally run government is inefficient
and unproductive, much less corrupt. However, it should not
come as a surprise to see them use state governments as a
sacrificial lamb to support the federal government bureaucracy they so love. I would submit to this editorial board that
*the larger a centrally run, hierarchically organized bureaucracy, the
more inefficient and unproductive the bureaucracy, until it reaches
an ultimate point where it becomes almost totally unresponsive and
corrupt.* When you add to this a monopoly status over entire
industries, such as education, the condition could not get
any worse. And, just to be clear, I define a monopoly as a
controlled market where people are forced to pay for the
product or service even if they choose not to use it.

A Pinch of Red Herring

Another tactic is to simply state a position or statistical
fact that is totally unrelated or irrelevant with the specific
goal of diverting attention or creating a distraction from
the position or issue. This type of non sequitur is commonly

referred to as a *red herring* (8). The term derives from the sport of fox hunting. A dried herring, which happens to be red, is dragged across a trail to distract dogs from the scent of the fox. The Latin name is *ignoratio elenchi*, which means "ignorance of refutation" (9). In simple terms, this means ignorance of the conclusion that one is trying to refute with the strategy being to ignore it or to change the focus to something else. The belief behind a red herring is that you win the argument by changing the subject. And of course, the more emotion associated with the red herring, the better. A simple example of a red herring is as follows: If I state a position that advocates reducing government spending as a means of reducing debt and improving the health of the economy and the opposing argument is focused on how someone voted in a previous election or who a previous president was, this is clearly a red herring that has absolutely nothing to do with debating the underlying facts or logic associated with the position. It may drive an emotional response and take the discussion off topic, and perhaps that is what is was designed to do. But it has nothing to do with the original position or debating any of the foundational points that support the position. Even if one is able to change the subject, and perhaps even succeed in debating the new topic or supporting the new position, it still does not alter the underlying factors associated with the original position.

Mix in a Straw Man

Another commonly used tactic in political discourse is the straw man argument, a specific type of red herring based on presenting a distorted representation of an opposing position and then attacking it. The name, as it implies, is based on establishing a position that is easily attacked and defeated (the straw man). The problem is that the straw man does not accurately represent the position of the person or group being attacked. A commonly used example that we have discussed in this book is as follows:

> *Government helps people. People against additional government spending are uncaring and lacking in compassion.*

The intent of this is to provoke the desired emotional response and shift the focus to the subjective debate of who cares the most. If the focus of the debate can be shifted to comparing the level of caring, then nobody will focus on whether government is actually effective and efficient at helping people. People that don't support continued growth of government are not the selfish, uncaring lot that they are commonly portrayed as through this straw man. They simply believe that there are more effective ways of helping people and improving society than through big government love. It is much easier, if you are an advocate of big government, to shift the focus from the effectiveness and productivity of government as compared to alternative approaches to something that generates an emotional response and can be more easily debated.

A straw man example can be found from the same newspaper editorial board mentioned previously, which wrote a recent editorial that reviewed the proposed "careless" House of Representatives budget, which it called "extreme" because the budget would dare cut any of the sacred big government programs and attempt to reform the big government entitlements that this newspaper cherishes (10). The article is filled with straw man distortions of the positions in the proposal and the horrible things that "could" happen as a result and concludes, predictably, that these extreme cuts would negatively impact the economy. They contrast this dastardly proposal with the approach they claim will protect their sacred big government programs and reduce the deficit by raising the level of confiscation on the "rich." Once again, supporters of big government go to the well of additional confiscation to continue with the unsustainable rate of government spending that will somehow result in the protection of sacred programs, debt reduction, and economic growth. They predictably rely on the false assumption that confiscating additional wealth from the rich will offset the additional spending that they advocate, despite the overwhelming evidence to the contrary.

Let It Bake

One of the most egregious examples that I have ever seen in leveraging many of the tactics presented in this chapter to justify big government love was the May 5, 2011, column in the *USA Today* by Sally Kohn (11). This column is actually one huge red herring with multiple embedded false assumptions, and a straw man or two to boot. Kohn attempts to justify a high government debt load by comparing the ratio of government debt to GDP with the ratio of debt to income of private companies. The fact that the purpose of the entire article is to distract the reader from the impact of the skyrocketing national debt makes it a red herring. The faulty comparison of the ratio of government debt to GDP with the ratio of debt to income of private companies, as a means to justify high government debt, is a blatant non sequitur. Her attempt to establish a ratio of government debt to the entire gross domestic product of the United States economy implies that she believes that the federal government is responsible for economic production and that gross domestic product represents what the government "earns." This takes the term *false assumption* to new heights. Since the government does not produce profit, it does not "earn" anything. Kohn's comparison of the $14.5 trillion in GDP to the present debt ($16 trillion) constitutes a roughly one-to-one ratio of debt-to-income, which she compares favorably to a number of United States-based private companies. Even if you used the government's revenue figure of $2.3 trillion, you would still have a ridiculously high level of debt. Kohn then proceeds to make the argument that government borrowing is equivalent to investing. The definition of investing requires some form of measurable return on the money put in. The better analogy would be to equate government borrowing to government spending where a clear one-to-one correlation exists. Kohn also attempts to link the government education monopoly to the success of Silicon Valley. Once again, the strongly held belief comes to the surface that people in the private sector that are successful are only successful because of big government. She summarizes by serving up a straw man that states that critics of big government say that government should be run like efficient, productive businesses. This is a misrepresentation, as the truth is that big government can't be run like an efficient, productive business per all of the underlying drivers and supporting examples previously presented in this book. Big government never has been run in an efficient and productive manner and, in the context of the private economy, it never will be. The position of many of those who oppose the view point taken by Kohn and others, is that the role of big government in the economy should be minimized, so that it has the least negative impact possible on the economy and the financial well-being of the private citizens of the country and the country overall.

But It's Complicated

The ultimate fallback position in support of big government is the idea that the economy is extremely complex or complicated and only the government is capable of fully understanding and managing it. This assumption, once again, leads down the familiar path that ends with more confiscation and bigger government. This false assumption is linked to the premise that big government, and the lawyers that run it, is smarter. The question that you often hear asked is "what is the government doing to improve the economy?" This question assumes that the government is fully capable of improving the economy, and it is simply a matter of the politicians in charge making the right choices and decisions on spending, regulating, and developing and enacting the right legislation. The reality is that the more the government encroaches on economic activity, the more the government distorts market forces, the less efficient markets become and, the more harm is inflicted on the economy and the citizenry overall. The economy may be complex but linking that statement to the need for a more active government role in the economy and for increased government spending and confiscation of revenue is not logical. The government's primary role with regards to the economy is the protection of the property rights of its citizens. When it ventures beyond this primary area of responsibility, the result is almost always incrementally negative when it comes to the economy. And yes, it is that simple.

CHAPTER 7

Avoiding the Abyss

I hope we have once again reminded people that man is not free unless government is limited. There's a clear cause and effect here that is as neat and predictable as a law of physics: as government expands, liberty contracts. — Ronald Reagan

How do we grow our economy, create opportunities, and increase the standard of living for our children and grandchildren? How do we, as a country, address the problem of runaway government spending and unsustainable debt? How does our country avoid hurtling into the abyss of insolvency and bankruptcy? The first step is to properly frame the problem in a way that people can easily understand. That is the primary purpose of this book. Understanding the problem requires that people also grasp its scope and magnitude. We can then work together to chart a new course. Without a dramatic change in course, our country is rapidly heading toward insolvency and bankruptcy. This chapter will explore some practical ideas for avoiding the abyss.

Changing the Context

Let us start by resetting the context and parameters of the debate. For the past forty years, the debate has centered on the questions of how much additional money we should spend and what we should spend it on. We are at a crossroads where the fundamental questions need to change. The idea that the United States, being $16 trillion in debt and borrowing forty cents on every dollar spent, can continue to spend above and beyond an upwardly adjusted floor from the previous year's spending, which is known as baseline budgeting, is a nonstarter. The broad shoulders of the private economy can no longer bear the weight of big government love.

Any government representative of the people who believes that baseline budgeting is a proper context for dealing with the country's fiscal crisis is mathematically challenged and needs to be voted out of office as soon as possible. For those who believe that the debate should focus on any spending increase whatsoever from the previous year's budget, they also clearly don't understand the depth of the problem and also need to be jettisoned. The debate with regards to the financial health of the United States needs to shift to a focus on how much government spending needs to be cut and where. Once again, when using the term *cut*, the reference is to how much less we are going to spend this year than what we spent last year. This fundamental change in mindset will go a long way to reversing the damage and the crushing debt burden that has been created over the last forty years.

First Steps

A logical first step in a process of change would be the elimination of the underlying mechanism that makes it next to impossible to cut spending—that would be the baseline budgeting requirement of the Congressional Budget and Impoundment Control Act of 1974, discussed in Chapter 3. This law needs to be replaced with a zero-based budgeting provision that forces government to build and justify their budgets from the ground up, starting from zero.

A positive next step would be the development of plans and budgets that emphasize minimizing, or limiting, the role of government in the economy. This is built on the following foundation as presented in this book:

- You can't spend money you don't have.
- Government is an inefficient and unproductive allocator and consumer of capital; therefore, capital extracted from private individuals, private businesses, or future generations and moved into the public sector will negatively impact the economy and the overall economic health of the nation.
- New laws and regulations must be designed to facilitate competition and reduce government's burden on the economy, not create additional costs, impediments, and market distortions.

Reversing the Flow of Capital

By reversing the trend of confiscating capital from private individuals, businesses, and from future generations in the form of debt to fund big government, the economy will once again begin to grow and prosper in a healthy manner. The result of healthy economic growth will be more jobs, higher wages, a higher overall standard of living, and ultimately, more revenue going into the government, which should be used to pay down the debt.

The idea that moving capital from the public sector to the private sector as a means for driving economic growth is not novel or new. The most recent example of the effectiveness of this approach was Ronald Reagan's presidency. During Reagan's two terms in office, from 1981 to 1989, income confiscation by the federal government was cut across the board, the number of regulations were cut, and there was at least an attempt to keep government spending in check, although this was a failed attempt, as at the time you had a Congress, which much like today, was determined to spend every penny they could and then some. During Reagan's term, more than sixteen million new jobs were created and the amount of revenue collected by the federal government and state governments increased despite dramatic cuts in tax rates (1). Yes, you read that correctly, Reagan cut tax rates and the amount of taxes collected by the government substantially increased. Reagan's term was also the trigger for a twenty-year period of rapid growth in which the revenue to government more than tripled despite the reduction in tax rates. Growth in revenue generated by the economy and collected by the government (federal, state, and local) during this period is illustrated in the following chart (2).

Figure 3—Government Total Revenue from
FY 1980 to FY 2000

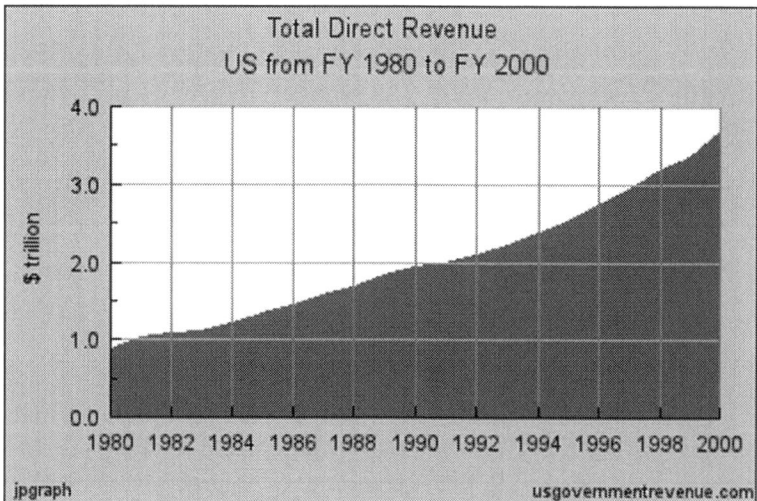

When you reverse the process of confiscating money from the private sector and moving it into big government, the government actually ends up with more money. This seems counterintuitive, but if you think about it in the context of what drives economic growth, it is rather obvious. Because the private markets are more productive and efficient, the rate of economic growth is increased. When the economy grows, the total amount of revenue that the government collects grows, even if it is a smaller percentage rate. The bottom line is that a smaller percentage of a larger, growing pie turns out to be much greater than a larger percentage of a stagnant or shrinking pie. This is why an emphasis on cutting government spending and reducing the amount of money confiscated from the private sector will result in economic growth and ultimately, a reduction in government debt.

While on the topic, let's address the emotional non sequiturs that invariably arise every time the name Ronald Reagan is mentioned. The one I hear most frequently is how Reagan actually raised taxes. Yes, the fact is that Reagan did raise certain taxes during his presidency. The deficit and overall debt grew under Reagan, as he was not able to control the voracious spending appetite of the Congress. This, however, doesn't deny the fact that tax rates and overall taxes, in aggregate, were dramatically decreased during his terms in office and he not only reversed a declining economy left by his predecessor but he triggered a transformative period of economic growth and prosperity. This red herring, thrown out by Reagan detractors, is simply designed to distract from, and diminish, Reagan's historical accomplishments.

Real Spending Cuts

A common refrain of big government lovers is that you can't have lower taxes and fatter government coffers. Well, sure you can, if the government cuts spending. The less of a drag the government places on the economy, the more efficient the economy, and the more money the government stands to collect. If the government stops continuously growing at an unsustainable rate, its coffers will eventually grow to be plenty fat. Once again, proponents of big government always leave spending cuts out of the choice of options when it comes to framing a decision or a debate. You must choose, but cutting the size of bloated government is never one of the choices.

When considering government spending cuts, nothing should be left off the table, including defense and entitlement programs. Entitlement programs, as they exist today, are clearly unsustainable and are in need of restructuring. With regards to entitlement programs that impact senior citizens, there are multiple options and proposals for restructuring these programs without impacting the benefits of those citizens who are already retired—our parents. The restructuring must occur in order for these programs to be sustainable for those still in the workforce. The deal is fairly simple: fundamentally reengineer the program for those of us who are still working or it won't exist in ten years when we approach retirement.

Each department of the federal government needs to be reevaluated with a goal of determining if the particular department is even relevant and required. The mission, goals, objectives, and costs of each department should be reviewed with the onus put on the department to justify its value and existence. Government priorities must be reset. When you borrow from future generations at the rate of forty cents on every dollar you spend, dramatic cuts must be made. Another positive step would be streamlining and simplifying the tax code. Eliminating most, if not all, deductions and implementing a flat income tax would not only simplify the tax code, it could also drive a reduction in the total amount of wages confiscated from the taxpayer. A side benefit would include eliminating much of the IRS and dramatically reducing the filing costs associated with taxes by enabling tax returns to be filed using a simple card or one page form.

Breaking Down Barriers: Market Inefficiencies and Distortions

Eliminating barriers that prevent the market from working in an efficient and optimal manner should become standard practice for improving the economy. Before determining barriers that are candidates for elimination, we should start by eliminating the habit of continuously constructing new barriers to a healthy market. In addition to understanding perceived benefits to citizens and the country as a whole, all new proposed laws and regulations should require a cost-benefit analysis that not only analyzes and determines the impact and cost on business and the economy but also establishes metrics so that these costs can be measured and tracked. As discussed previously, new regulations should facilitate a healthy economic environment versus creating excessive new burdens on business and new opportunities to line the pockets of the legal community.

Market Distortions: Healthcare

Breaking down barriers requires a relentless search for the causes of market inefficiencies and distortions along with a determination to make positive changes. Healthcare provides an example of a clear and immediate opportunity. A primary challenge of the healthcare system is managing costs, while maintaining and improving quality, for a growing and aging population. The best way to control costs is to promote competition and drive efficiency. By passing legislation to effectively take over the industry, the government is heading in the opposite direction. This will only lead to inefficient service, increased government spending, and increased debt. Does anyone really believe that the federal government can efficiently and productively manage the healthcare industry, which accounts for approximately one sixth of the overall economy? Does anyone really believe that the cost of healthcare will be reduced and the quality of healthcare improved by having big government running it?

There are a many steps that could be taken to facilitate healthcare improvements, without increased government involvement. My goal here is not to attempt to fix the healthcare system, but simply to offer a few ideas that could potentially lead to incremental improvements. Government, through the Food and Drug Administration (FDA), indirectly promotes patented synthetic drugs through their drug approval process. By approving a patented synthetic drug, the government gives a pharmaceutical company an exclusive right to sell that drug on the market for up to twenty years. That exclusivity eliminates competition for the particular synthetic drug over the defined period of time. This allows the pharmaceutical companies that develop these drugs to potentially generate large profits and invest a portion of that profit in research and development of new drugs. In some cases, competition could be driven, however, from naturally occurring foods, herbs, supplements, and other chemical substances that are not synthetically produced. Items that occur in nature and are not synthetically produced cannot be patented. Therefore, they are not aggressively promoted and marketed for their healthcare benefits. The pharmaceutical industry does not get paid big money to tell you that a naturally occurring ingredient in pineapples may reduce arthritis inflammation, or that cherries may help with the symptoms of gout, or probiotics may improve digestion, which could positively impact a wide range of ailments. Additionally, alternative, less-expensive healthcare approaches, which can benefit many, such as chiropractic and acupuncture are only partially covered, if at all, by insurance plans. The big money is made by promoting a synthetic drug that has been patented and approved by the FDA or by having a medical test run on a piece of equipment that has FDA certification. These are simply the drivers based on how the system has been designed. With some investigation and research, enabled by the Internet, health management and wellness through less expensive, natural means is now accessible and available to many. However, it is certainly not enabled or promoted by the present-day system. I am not suggesting that the government should not have a role in reviewing and approving new drugs and medical equipment for the purpose of protecting the safety of its citizens. I am suggesting, however, that creating new restrictions and impediments, like the government discouraging the promotion of the benefits of naturally occurring products, only serves to protect the status quo and artificially raise the overall cost of healthcare in certain instances. The idea that a naturally occurring product would have to go through an FDA certification process in order to make a health claim, which many are now suggesting, is a specific example of this.

Another example of government imposing barriers to progress in healthcare is the expansion of the government's role in reviewing and approving modern communication technologies. Many new technologies, which are widely used in other industries and by consumers, provide the foundation for efficient, innovative healthcare processes by enabling a variety of healthcare-related devices to transmit data and information remotely. These technologies enable broader collaboration between healthcare providers and caregivers, along with new delivery models. The solution to the healthcare dilemma lies in greater transparency, easier access to information, streamlining government's role in the industry, and creating a more level playing field that promotes and encourages innovation and competition.

The fact that many healthcare consumers are one step removed from the actual costs of the goods and services also serves to distort the market and impede competition. Because businesses get a tax deduction, they pay for the health insurance of their employees, typically passing on only a portion of the cost to their employees through payroll deductions. This creates a disincentive for the consumer to shop and compare prices for healthcare goods and services. Studies have shown that costs are reduced for people that have high deductible insurance plans (3). When people are forced to reach into their pocket and pay directly for a good or service, they tend to pay more attention to the cost, which ultimately puts pressure on pricing. The business deduction for employee health insurance, along with the payroll deduction of the employee's portion of the insurance cost, tends to insulate the consumer from the direct costs of healthcare. A potential solution that has been suggested in the past would be to eliminate the tax deduction for businesses and provide the consumer with some form of a tax credit. Increasing the exposure of the consumer to the actual pricing of the goods and services that they are consuming will serve to increase the efficiency of the market.

Another opportunity is to eliminate barriers that restrict competition among health insurance providers. Preventing insurance companies from selling health insurance across state lines is one example of such a barrier. Technology is enabling a new connected era where one's location will not prevent a patient from being able to communicate and collaborate with doctors and other caregivers, regardless of physical location. If physical location is no longer an impediment, why do we impose rules and regulations that artificially create restrictions and constraints? If we desire an effective, efficient, and productive marketplace that drives a vibrant economy, we must facilitate and enable markets by eliminating needless or outdated restrictions.

Market Distortions: Labor

Additional examples of government introducing distortions into the market can be found in the continuous attempts by government to control labor costs by mandating wage scales that big government believes to be "fair" (there goes that word again). Invariably, the market always responds to market distortions in ways that the government rarely anticipates. In the case of minimum-wage laws, hiring is decreased, especially among the young and new entrants into the labor pool who most need the experience. In the case of expanding prevailing wage laws, like the Davis-Bacon Act of 1931 (4), in which the government artificially inflates the cost of labor, the overall costs of government projects are driven up, making an inefficient model even more inefficient. The ultimate example of government distorting labor costs, however, is the unionization of government workers. What is the purpose of unions? I always thought it was to protect the "little guy" from those big, evil, profit-driven corporations. But why would anyone need protection from loving big government who only has the best interests of everyone in mind? I have nothing against unions and certainly recognize the important role that they have played in our nation's history. I also believe that people who join unions in the private sector deal with the same challenges and market forces that everyone else working in the private sector has to deal with. If you work in the private sector and want to join a union to bargain collectively, or for whatever other reason, good for you. In the private sector, your interests are inextricably linked to the interests of the company for which you work, regardless of whether you are in a union. If the company you work for is unable to generate profit and survive, people lose their jobs. However, when you work for the government, which has no profit motive and operates under a different set of rules and drivers, unionization and collective bargaining is clearly a conflict of interest. By having a vested interest in big government and large pay packages and benefits that are not market-driven, public sector unions use money confiscated from taxpayers to lobby against the best interests of the taxpayers—that would be for even bigger and more costly big government. And that is the very definition of conflict of interest. Public sector unions are able to directly influence and choose who they negotiate and bargain with through lobbying and direct financing of their chosen candidates. Their employer, that being the government, runs a monopoly and when unionized public sector workers gain the power to determine their boss, they have effectively circumvented the interests of those who are forced to pay the bills and absorb the distorted costs of their labor. President Franklin Roosevelt drew a line when it came to unionization of government workers: "Meticulous attention," the president insisted in 1937, "should be paid to the special relations and obligations of public servants to the public itself and to the Government. . . . The process of collective bargaining, as usually understood, cannot be transplanted into the public service." Roosevelt believed that "[a] strike of public employees manifests nothing less than an intent on their part to obstruct the operations of government until their demands are satisfied. Such action looking toward the paralysis of government by those who have sworn to support it is unthinkable and intolerable." (5) When taxpayers attempt to fix this clearly broken model, the government union simply ratchets up the pressure, as demonstrated recently in Wisconsin and other states.

Summary

A summary of suggested actions that would facilitate a positive change in course are as follows:

1) Properly frame and understand the debate and problem.
2) Change the context of the debate from "what we should spend on and how much" to "what we should cut and by how much."
3) Change the underlying government budgeting mechanism known as baseline budgeting, which prevents cuts in government spending.
4) Reduce the amount of money government confiscates from private individuals and businesses.
5) Actually cut government spending in a significant manner.
6) Develop a relentless focus on breaking down barriers that impede an efficient private marketplace.

Minimizing the government's involvement in the free market, reducing the cost of government in the economy, and implementing reforms that will facilitate the proper function of private markets will ensure a growing vibrant economy for generations to come.

Back Where We Started

Do you still have that dollar bill that was discussed at the beginning of our journey? Let's ask the question one last time: Who is more capable of making the decision on what should be done with that dollar bill, the dollar bill that your neighbor is holding, or the dollar bill that your children and grandchildren someday will be holding? Who should make that decision? You, your neighbor, your child, or your loving big government? Sustaining or increasing government's present role in the economy requires that the government confiscate and spend more of your money. This assumes that the impact of the confiscation and spending will be more positive than if the government did not confiscate your money and you were allowed to make the decision on how your money should be allocated. Think about that next time you hear a politician come up with a great idea on how to best spend yours or someone else's money.

END

NOTES

Introducing Big Government LOVE

1. http://forecast-chart.com/forecast-national-debt.html

2. Ibid

3. http://www.usgovernmentrevenue.com/yearrev2011_0.html

4. http://www.cbpp.org/cms/index.cfm?fa=view&id=1258

What a Drag: Big Government and the Economy

1. Creative Destruction was introduced by Joseph Schumpter (1883-1950) to describe the process of free markets.

2. http://www.merriam-webster.com/

3. Ibid

4. http://www.usgovernmentspending.com/

5. ibid

6. http://www.tradingeconomics.com/united-states/gdp-growth

7. http://fire.pppl.gov/fy12_doe_summ.pdf

8. http://www.aaas.org/spp/rd/xxvi/chap9.htm

9. http://www.google.com/publicdata/explore?ds=z8o7pt6rd5uqa6_&met_y=unemployment_rate&idim=country:el&fdim_y=seasonality:sa&dl=en&hl=en&q=unemployment+rate+in+greece

10. http://www.guardian.co.uk/business/2012/apr/16/european-youth-unemployment-soars?newsfeed=true

11. http://epp.eurostat.ec.europa.eu/statistics_explained/index.php/Structure_of_government_debt

12. http://www.publicserviceeurope.com/article/1727/demands-for-austerity-pushing-spain-to-the-brink#axzz1sEquEg5u

13. http://www.whitehouse.gov/sites/default/files/omb/assets/legislative_reports/us_contributions_to_the_un_06062011.pdf

14. http://www.heritage.org/research/reports/2012/04/the-history-of-the-bloated-un-budget-how-the-us-can-rein-it-in

15. http://www.foxnews.com/projects/pdf/091709_overview.pdf

16. ibid

17. http://www.un.org/en/documents/charter/preamble.shtml

18. http://www.charitywatch.org/criteria.html

19. http://climateclips.com/archives/271

20. http://www.tollroadsnews.com/node/5689

21. Ibid

22. Ibid

23. http://www.ntu.org/tax-basics/who-pays-income-taxes.html

Planting the Seed: The Congressional Budget Act of 1974

1. http://www.gpo.gov/fdsys/pkg/GPO-RIDDICK-1992/pdf/GPO-RIDDICK-1992-34.pdf

2. http://www.usgovernmentspending.com/

Laws and Lawyers: Big Government and Big Business

1. http://www.wisegeek.com/what-percent-of-the-us-population-do-lawyers-comprise.htm

2. http://archive.sba.gov/advo/research/rs264tot.pdf

3. http://www.forbes.com/sites/waynecrews/2011/07/06/the-cost-of-government-regulation-the-barack-obama-cass-sunstein-urban-legend/

Straw Men and Non Sequiturs and Red Herrings! Oh, My!

1. Wall Street Journal, The Facts About Fracking, June 25, 2011

2. http://www.pacificlegal.org/page.aspx?pid=1612

3. http://www.merriam-webster.com/

4. Ibid

5. President Obama March 31, 2012 weekly address

6. Ibid

7. N.Y. Times, Editorial of the Times, The States Get a Poor Report Card, March, 20,2012

8. http://www.merriam-webster.com/

9. http://www.fallacyfiles.org/redherrf.html

10. N.Y. Times, Editorial of the Times, The Careless House Budget, March 21, 2012

11. USA Today, Don't believe the hype about our national debt, Sally Kohn, May 25, 2011

Avoiding the Abyss

1. http://www.cato.org/publications/commentary/jobscreation-lesson-past

2. http://www.usgovernmentrevenue.com/revenue_chart_1950_2015USr_13s1li011mcn_F0t

3. http://www.rand.org/news/press/2011/03/25.html

4. http://www.dol.gov/compliance/laws/comp-dbra.htm

5. http://ofbuckleyandbeatles.wordpress.com/2011/02/21/the-trouble-with-public-sector-unions/

Made in the USA
Charleston, SC
04 September 2012